Zippy's Lost Stripes

Brad Herzog

Illustrated by Michele Noiset

Harcourt Achieve

Rigby • Saxon • Steck-Vaughn

www.HarcourtAchieve.com
1.800.531.5015

Zippy was resting by the tree as a group of beautiful zebras walked by. "Hello," she said, "I like your stripes."

"Thank you!" one of the zebras said. "Where are your stripes?"

When Zippy looked down, she noticed that she didn't have any stripes!

Zippy decided to visit her friend, Whiskers,
who had a lot of stripes.
"Whiskers, where are my stripes?"
she asked.

4

"I don't know," said Whiskers.
"Maybe you should look for your stripes
in the city."

Zippy rode the bus to the city,
where she saw all kinds of stripes.
She saw red and white stripes
on a flag.

The penguin twins, Pim and Pongo Pippen, were wearing hats and ties with pink and purple stripes.

While Zippy was walking, she found
a candy store.
She saw some big, striped candy canes
hanging in the window.
"Do you have any stripes for me?"
she asked.

Razz, the owner of the store, said,
"I have a lot of candy with stripes.
But I can't take the stripes off of
the candy, of course!"

At Pixie's Barber Shop, there were
red and white stripes on the pole.
"Have you seen my stripes?" Zippy asked.

Pixie didn't answer.
She was too busy cutting hair.

Zippy kept searching.
She saw a football field
with big, white stripes on the grass.
The two teams playing football
were wearing uniforms that had stripes
on them.

Zippy saw the referee, who was wearing a shirt with black and white stripes. "Are those my stripes?" Zippy asked.

"No," said the referee, "these stripes are on my shirt!"

Zippy kept walking, and she saw her friend, Hobie, sitting on a park bench.
She told him about her search for her lost stripes.

Hobie looked at Zippy and smiled.
"I know why you don't have stripes,"
he said.
"You're not a zebra.
You're a beautiful white horse!"

"At last, I understand!" Zippy said.
"I don't need stripes.
I'm fine just the way I am!"